HAIKU CHIAROSCURO

Lighter and Darker Sides
of Haiku Poetry and Prose

David Cobb

2015

2015 Equinox Press

© 2015 David Cobb

All rights reserved. No part of this book
may be used or reproduced without written
permission of the author except in the case
of brief quotations embodied in critical articles
and reviews. The author may be contacted at
email@davidcobb.co.uk

ISBN 978-0-9566833-2-8

Equinox Press
Sinodun Shalford Braintree Essex CM7 5HN UK

www.davidcobb.co.uk

CONTENTS

Totem	1
Japanese Roulette	2
60 Andrassy Boulevard	4
Leise, Leise	6
Fearing	8
Kafka-ku	10
The Thin Line Between 'Moment' and 'Momentum'	12
Boxtel, July 1945	14
Goslar, September 1945	15
Doing Eggs	16
Lightning Years	17
Casting a Cold Eye	18
Memories Shared with a Topiary Dodo	20
Moving Sheep	22
On the Red Button	24
Pillow Talk	26
Hi-Ho, Hi-Ho, 'tis Off ...	28
The Pastry Board	29
Knowing Mouse	30
The Drift from Must	32
Green Woman	35
Dark Margins	38
Garden of Forgetfulness	40
Acknowledgments	42

TOTEM

Behold, within a huge Japanese barrel
Hokusai's cooper,
shrunken small, an oyster workman
employed in spring-shaving his shell.
Naked, except for the knotted
rag of cloth in his groin.

Naked as William Blake
reading aloud and nude in his Lambeth yard
and Mrs Blake, summoned like Eve
to come, bare, and play midwife
to verses sticky with afterbirth,
however neighbours might mutter
about his messages from angels.

On the horizon within the barrel
Hokusai has tucked Fuji-san,
leaving us to recognise it
as his totem.

    watercolour
    a wash blue as rain
    wet to the eye

JAPANESE ROULETTE

on the balcony
still in her night robe
Fuji in mist

        sunrise
        the cockerel's wattles
        on fire

fish stall
rucking for their heads
a bowl of eels

        puffer fish
        their faces exhibiting
        some uncertainty

footsteps
light as shudders
on the nightingale floor

      rouge flowers
      she names them and picks one
      with a blush

earthquake tremor
    the municipal gardener
    draws back his hoe

      two-inch *futon*
          and all beneath it
          Hiroshima

60 ANDRASSY BOULEVARD

is a fine Neo-Renaissance mansion
on a fine broad avenue
lined with plane trees
in Budapest.
It has now the name 'House of Terrors',
a museum commemorating the years
when it was headquarters
of 'state protection'.

Here, for seven years, reigned Pétér Gabór
until one day, at a state reception,
to his great amazement
handcuffs snapped around his wrists
and his masters informed him,
'the game is over'.

registration
three paces on all sides
rough brick walls

                                      box files
                                      a ten foot long stack
                                      for letter A

spiral stairs
the giddiness
of spectres

                    in the beatings cell
                    middle of the floor
                    a choked-up drain

torture chamber
walls worn away
by a sponge

                    hangman's rope
                    coiled as a serpent coils
                    when it has fed

LEISE, LEISE *

swing *leise, leise*
a lad who looks far too old
to play on swings

                        seesaw
            each side the tipping point
                    a hairy leg

On coffee shop tables
crumbs, smears,
cups not cleared away
before the dark clouds burst
and filled them to
overflowing,
stains leaking out onto table cloths.
Paper cloths,
waitresses crumple them
in the palm of one hand.

leise: German/Yiddish for 'quietly'

A man, a statue of a man,
lies on his back
one arm upraised and pointing
into a sick-looking tree's
overhanging
dusty canopy of leaves;

a knee bent double
as if he would like to rise
but is anchored
to the paving
by the buckle of his belt
or maybe braces.

And a small boy running by
breaks step for a moment
to shake that upraised hand
and then runs on.

                    Old Jewish Quarter
                    kids with backs to the wall
                            a game of tag

FEARING

        a glint of sunlight
     caught by copper tongs
        in a dusty grate

By the fireside, perched on its rim at a jaunty but
almost perilous angle, a cone of white plaster on
a small round plinth of yew. Gouged out of its
plaster face, a whirl of wrinkles penetrating to
its heart. As often it sets me thinking of her ...

This sculpture she made for Keats' Bicentenary
one mid-June, in the garden of his house in
Hampstead. The inspiration for it was his sonnet
When I have fears that I may cease to be ...

        Midsummers' Night
     a white face haunting
        the mulberry

That was before the cancer took hold
in her breast, before she found herself
on her own with two growing boys to raise,
before she reverted to her maiden name.
Oh, then she had fears that she would cease
to be, fears never spoken, but I knew
when her tears wet my shirt.

I cast those dark memories aside in her familiar laugh, how she would tell me of some prank in her free-and-easy days. How once, in Ireland, in a circus, she had stood in when the usual stooge had walked out on the knife-throwing act. All the way round the gypsy thrower had stitched her body to the board through her scanty dress. Fears then of 'ceasing to be', surely, but not daring to tremble.

Reward? The gypsy gave her a stuffed giraffe. Ten or more feet tall. She lugged it onto the night ferry to Holyhead, hitch-hiked with it to London, could not get it through the door where she lodged. The giraffe ever since loaned out to some grand stately house in Derbyshire.

Making life-size heads of camels from clay, that was my folly, and in her pottery classes she showed me how. Pieced together my first one when, in the kiln, it shattered. Did not hold me back when, having made a whole portfolio of camels, my fancy turned to the rhino. She drew pictures for some of my poems, married a minor poet, we lost touch, I never dared to ask ...

        solstice shadows
        a shiver passes
    through the sculpture cone

KAFKA-KU *

as each car parks
he dips a hopeful mop
the migrant worker

                                        litter bin
                                        wrapped in cling film
                                        the searching hand

kale field
the gang boss busy as ever
with his thumbs

                                        dealers in futures
                                        the brass plate above
                                        two cardboard sheets

outside the food bank
the man who never read
Robin Hood

homing at nightfall
the charcoal caws
of rooks

                        smouldering pyre
                        the flap of vultures'
                        ancient wings

neglected tomb centuries old the ivy he rips

* *"... characteristic of Kafka's work is the portrayal of an enigmatic reality, in which the individual is seen as lonely, perplexed, and threatened."*
The Oxford Companion to English Literature, 1967

ku: the element in *haiku* which means 'poem'

THE THIN LINE BETWEEN "MOMENT" AND "MOMENTUM"

the moment 'expected'
turns
to 'landed'

                        trolleys colliding
                        at each aisle corner
                        she says it's fate

Folkestone funicular
a couple with eyes glued
to the moon

                    flung-open windows
                        snips of toenails
                          taking flight at dawn

rooting out couch grass
      Everest, he hears,
         has moved three inches

sunshine and shadow
the way our SatNav
will not have us go

        rejection slip
        the postman checks his watch
        by the cuckoo clock

seeing off her train
    no kiss till the guard
    blows his whistle

        meeting
        the new neighbours
        thanks to their 'lost' cat

scattering ashes
the odd places he fancied
roundabouts and wells

BOXTEL, JULY 1945

Well, yes, like a burr it sticks to me,
the Netherlandish name, because that day
of crawling heat our troop train slowed
and stopped dustily at Boxtel, no great shock,
for in a land of rubbled recognition
there were no bearings, schedule or a clock.

One of us eased the strap and let
the window down, perhaps to ascertain
why, from the mob of smokers, not a sound
arose. Just hands from pockets drawn
spoke of no purpose to get on the train.

I chose one head, a ripe blond sheaf of corn,
and motioned to the boy, some nine years old,
how in the butty taken from my lips
there was still meat. And felt his hand
as with no awkwardness he laid in mine
two clogs of his own making, painted gold.

GOSLAR, SEPTEMBER 1945

This is how peace returns: a man with drums
beats three beats to the bar with his right hand
and taps the counterpoint, not with his left,
but with a stick bound to a stump of arm.

The *Kursaal,* short a notch or two of heat,
is filled with *Frauen* tapping with their feet.
Coffee and biscuits of *Ersatz* content
are in the interval their frugal treat.

Is this how normality returns? A stray
khaki soldier, latterly at war,
learns operetta songs and breaks
crumbs from a chocolate bar.

DOING EGGS

My turn to make breakfast for two and my six-year-old grandson offers help. Never discourage a small Figaro.

'You know how to make scramble ...'

'Course I do!' before I end the question.

'... without breaking shells of any eggs?'

'You can't, grandpa. Just can't!'
A tone in his voice as if he thinks me gaga.
For he's already got plenty of common sense,
knows a bit about structures and strengths.
'I'll have to show you, then,' I say.

Take a needle, pierce an egg top and bottom,
blow out the yolk and globular white.
Just enough puff left in my lungs to do
something not done since I was a child myself.

Grandson watches me with accumulating scorn.
'If you can put it all back in, that will be real cool!'

                              one KBDs, one MICE
                              plurals that do not faze
                              a six-year-old

LIGHTNING YEARS

first winter
sticking his tongue out
to sleet

                              band in the park
                              out in his pushchair
                              trying to conduct

cemetery
he shows how his teacher showed
what they did to Christ

                              Christmas stocking
                              a gum shield for rugby
                              in the toe

CASTING A COLD EYE

> a field of flax
> so blue, so calm
> to sail the eye upon

Many haiku surface when the eye has 'gone sailing', with or without the mind as crew. Musicians have a saying, 'Good composers compose, great composers feel.'

Stuff. Haiku are distilled. Let's change the subject to William Butler Yeats, pacing up and down the main street of a Sussex village, composing the line he wished on his tombstone.

'Cast a cold eye, on life, on death.'

> watercress beds
> a spotted dog asleep
> on a painted barge

eve of the 'sparing'
lambs digging deep
for dam's teats

against the gale
cricket bat willows
toss

        solar eclipse
        the oncoming headlights
        do not dip

Monday morning
the neighbour sweeps leaves
with his windscreen wiper

        in eye sockets
        the thawed-out instincts
        of a dead white hare

MEMORIES SHARED WITH A TOPIARY DODO

shading the eyes
of the topiary dodo
my Van Gogh hat

        rush to the postbox
        the man in front of me
        on stilts

'Welcome to Purim!'
all the reception party
wear red noses

        singing me *Lieder*
        the cherry of her tongue
        with each high C

desert island discs
the geek who reads cuneiform
a fan of rap

under desert skies
stars that twinkle
on scarabs' backs
signalling dot-dot-dash,
'Mind, my dung ball!'

                      thunder spots
             some clouds must find it hard
                             to pour out rain

that Christmas gesture
neighbour and I both
with bottles of wine

                      polling station
                      the wall-eyed dog
                      chained to the door

referendum
the morning all is done
the toast still Burns

MOVING SHEEP

'Ho-up!' is a way they holler to sheep
up in the lea gap between steep fells
to unfamiliar ears sounding like 'Hope!'
but in the small word-stock of the flock
cue to return to the galvanised tin trough
for the pellet ration — their 'nine a day'.

If any ewe's laggardly or
of a mind to go where she will
they desist from 'Ho-up!',
get behind her with a stick,
make as if to prod her rump,
whistle to the wire-haired dog.

Driving sheep differs
from calling them in:
the slither of gumboots
through wet fell grass
is all the needed spur
behind the fat chumps of sheep
to set them running pell-mell
to pen or tether.
So it is one early day of frost
when a squeal into daylight
a black trailer parks in the drab lane,
lets down its desperate ramp
under grey alder trees,

and the whole flock is driven out
of the fold in the mire.

Just a quick glance
from cornered eyes at the stick
or the lolled-out tongue
of the black worrying dog
and the sheep all bundle ahead,
bleating, bleating, bleating,
no hope of hearing ever more
'Ho-up! Ho-up! Ho-up!'

ON THE RED BUTTON

the briefest lull
    in flowers of the field
    the seeds go pop

        on a plain of sand
        labelled with skulls
        the prospect of a crop
        as quick as cress

    as
womb-fruit
  the old bards
would have known them,
  mothers' sons all,
    soldiers
   who were
    hung
in this orange grove
from fruitless trees

        a man with a torch
        goes searching for a name
        the Menin Gate

Armistice Day
tying shoelaces
in double knots

        the red button
        not to miss the drones
        that didn't miss

Lovers' Lane
from a dud bomb the smell
of cordite sweat

PILLOW TALK

first jaunty day
the spurt of women's legs
from yellow dresses

                                      pair of blackbirds
                                      skeining twitters
                                        as they intertwine

testing the water
he up to his thighs
she to her ankles

moonlight taking time to wax her legs

pillow talk
the laws of cricket
about leg-before

                        back-lit
                        in the dawn light
                        her 'broken ends'

up in the attic
the stillness of moths
between thunderclaps

                        dark markings
                        flushed from the flower bed
                        a burnet moth

ravens plotting
new ways to be ominous
old castle walls

HI-HO, HI-HO, 'TIS OFF ...

rush hour train
in the nick of time
odd socks

                    coffee break
                    asking the new PA
                    if she takes sugar

revolving doors
between passing glances
shatterproof glass

              performance review
              the boss apologising
              milk not cream

THE PASTRY BOARD

Stuffed in the garden shed in all kinds weather,
its tenons but loose teeth, damp rot its grain,
at last it is no more than spider webs
liming one bit together with another.

Rout in the end: detaching from their frame
the four planks fall apart, a rabble only
fit for kindling of a paltry fire
to crackle and spit and tell hollow jokes.

Ah, the stories that go up in flames!
Of mother cutting stars from sheer white paste,
my hands wedging clay for clumsy pots,
or father with it easeled on his knees

painting nostalgia for the Chiltern Hills.
Such things were tolerated through pursed lips.
Mother would have been a hundred — no, more
like a hundred-and-twenty — when it fell to bits.

KNOWING MOUSE

      partners in crime
    behind dark shades no clue
     what she thinks of me

An in-service workshop for teachers of English
in Bangkok. Invited to be a resource, they pair
me with a young, very pretty woman to make
visual aids. We chat, in our two languages,
and slowly it dawns, she uses the Thai word *noo*,
the proper noun for 'mouse', as a pronoun, to
refer to herself, and also to address those she
thinks of as her social inferiors.

"Go, mouse, fetch me an iced coffee," instructing
a servant. Handing over a *baht* coin, she adds,
"Take care, mouse, not to spill it this time!"
And then, because people are beginning to
wonder why she is suddenly drinking coffee after
coffee, "Mouse couldn't sleep a wink last night."

Five afternoons mouse and I are employed
together, drawing and snipping, painting and
pasting, melting wax to fix things together.
The day after we disperse, there's a scandal
on the front pages of the newspapers.

With her photo. And briefly this story. A short time ago, when mouse was on a linguistics course, the professor had seduced her. Swore to her he meant to leave his wife, tired of living with a parrot, he said.

But then, on the very eve of our workshop together it must have been, she went on a seaside outing with friends, and there strolling on the beach, elbow nudging elbow, who but the professor and his wife. The old folk saying, 'The snake can see the hen's nipples, the hen can see the snake's feet.'

Gossip added detail to the bare report. When the sirens sounded and police burst into the school, the principal calmed them down. "Miss Sulee is teaching just now. Come back when lessons end for the day." And she gave the officers 'tea money' to go away.

In mouse's purse they found the pistol, wrapped neatly in rose-coloured silk. Were puzzled
by the other small metal thing in her purse.
I could have explained it to them.

> what to think of her
> using a bell with no tongue
> to snuff a candle

THE DRIFT FROM MUST

turning damp soil
robin and I see
eye to eye

                              back ache
                              the soothing touch
                              of pigeon coos

out of breath
step back and let the fence
do the groaning

                              topiary dodo
                              a watchful eye
                              on its growing feet

    walking party
    each picking out
    his own kind of stick

a four-leaf clover
it may have been — but the dog
pooped on it

        dry stone wall
        sunshine
        on the soles of boots

lucky horseshoe
in distant time the pocket
full of sugar lumps

        from the church organ
        on a Tuesday
        hurdy-gurdy tunes

no more than

half itself
the magpie in snow

GREEN WOMAN

>dandelion day
>not the brown sweater
>but the blue

I finish dressing as the letterbox downstairs
claps shut.

A white paper envelope, the address in familiar
aquamarine. No hint of any frailty there
though it would have been handwritten in bed
propped on three ample goose-down pillows.
How she spends most days, she told me.
Oh, can get out of bed a bit, bent over a stick,
her weight by her own estimation little more
than that of a swan, yet (as the doctor keeps on
warning her) enough to break a bone.

I open the envelope and separate the pages.

>a grey eyelash
>too light for gravity
>floats free

Ah, she's going to entertain me, put right some
of my suppositions about Nature, things I glibly
put into poems when I don't know the facts.

Like how dandelions have no sex life. Just clone.
Or the way the amazing Rothschild woman
discovered how many times a flea can jump in
sixty seconds. Did it with a drum. Or how high.
Several feet, apparently.

But no, today she's putting me straight about the
fellow of many visages who made her famous.
The Green Man.

Her golden time was when she was seeking him,
in his many guises, in many lands. Before she
became so fragile, but still able to clamber into
crannies and bat holes to take photographs.
Black-and-white. Her own man with his foot
wedged against the bottom rung of the ladder,
saying nothing that might intrude upon her
thoughts.

Warns me to ignore the theorists who associate
the Green Man with the Great Memory or the
Face of Glory. Has no time for them.

And here a salutation would end the letter except
a *pto* bids me turn to a *ps.* Odd coincidence,
says the *ps,* so unlikely she forgot to mention it.

A Japanese artist has written to her, he saw
her name and address in a membership list.

Longs to be in touch with her to share ideas,
for the Japanese too have a Green Man,
that he's sure about, and he employs this icon
in each one of his paintings. Just now has
an exhibition in a London gallery. Any chance
they could meet there?

What, and she lying crippled in a bed? Road and
rail totally ruled out. Her son has chartered a
helicopter.

And then a final closure: "Enjoy the spring, it's
come at last!"

        catkins
        the yellowing
        of Old Man's Beard

        catmint
        the new kitten's
        first deep breath

DARK MARGINS

The plane dips a wing towards Brazzaville.
There is a free seat between me and the
youngish woman by the window. Across
this divide, all the way from London we have
exchanged barely a word. Sometimes
a companionable glance, but her eyes mostly
shut during the flight.

Now they are suddenly wide open, she has
jerked herself forwards, her whole face lit up.
The dream of her life, she tells me, is about
to come true.

> *... for safety reasons*
> *ensure the person next to you*
> *is in upright position*

An epidemiologist, she clarifies herself.
From Puerto Rico. Bound for the headwaters
of the Congo. There to fill test tubes with local
sputum, spittle laced with a death-dealing virus
that has so far (and that is until the late
1970s let me advise you) kept all its secrets
from science. To me its name is new.

"And you?" she asks.

Comparisons shameful and I have to blush.
In an out of township schools, I say. Just
to sit at the back of classrooms and
observe lessons. Be critically observed myself,
probably, the only visiting White. Though
engagements are liable to last-minute
cancellation, as when one of 'Winnie's Boys',
a top class student, drops a loaded dustbin from
great height onto the head of the school principal
standing down below and the school is closed.

Otherwise, sitting tamely, barely aware which
township I happen to be in, watching and
listening, wondering at the number of people
queuing with empty pails outside the Mardi
Gras Offal Centre. My own feeble gesture,
to slip past the censors the song they ban,
We Shall Overcome.

    back of the class
    the girl with a weeping sore
    knows all the answers

GARDEN OF FORGETFULNESS

hayfield grasses
like old acquaintances
they wave to me

        the world
        turning much too fast
        spring gale in June

dandelion
the bumble bee rubs
its belly on it

        horizon
        of tall hedges
        lilac time

(at the Welsh Harp reservoir, Brent)

the bubbled breath of frogs by lily pads :
a brood of cygnets in a mute swan's wake

last sentence dotted
time to shake out cinders
from the toaster

        for thyme
        with its myriad florets
            an absence of bees

they grow anyway
    fuchsia and nemesia
    though I mix their names

        phew! thanks ...
           Thunderbird confirms
           I meant to do it

where nettles are king
arcane babble-babble
of the churchyard stream

ACKNOWLEDGEMENTS

The following first appeared in the on-line literary magazine *KYSO Flash Nos. 2/ 3*, North Carolina, USA, Feb and June 2015 respectively. I am grateful to the editor, Clare MacQueen for these: the poems *Boxtel, July 1945* and *Goslar, September 1945;* the haibun *Fearing, Doing Eggs,* and *Knowing Mouse* (the last of these noticed in *The Review Review.).*

The haibun *60 Andrassy Boulevard* appeared first in *Blithe Spirit Vol 25 No 1,* 2015. The 5 haiku on p. 10 were in *Blithe Spirit, Vol 25 No. 3,* 2015.

Stand-alone haiku appeared as follows: *earthquake tremor,* 2nd prize, *Mainichi Daily News* 17th annual contest, 2013; *dandelion, Presence* No 50, July 2014; *a man with a torch, Blithe Spirit,* Vol 20 No 3, 2010; *eclipse, Blithe Spirit* Vol 25 No 2, 2015; *Christmas stocking, Blithe Spirit* Vol 24 No 1, 2014; *no more than half itself* (here presented as the author's own haiga) awarded first prize in the *Itoen International Haiku Contest,* 2010; *watercress beds* gained an honourable mention in *Evening Breeze,* anthology of the *Janice M Bostok Haiku Awards,* pub. *Paper Wasp,* Queensland, Australia, 2012; *scattering ashes* appeared in the anthology, *The Humours of Haiku,* Iron Press, 2012.

Special mention of my Dutch friend, Max Verhart, who translated the poem *Boxtel, July 1945* into Dutch and arranged with the editor of *Brabants Centrum* (circulating in the Boxtel region) for it to be published there, in both Dutch and English versions, on 6 June 2014, a day celebrated annually in the Netherlands as National Liberation Day.

Also by David Cobb

Anchorage, foreword by Michael McClintock, pub. Red Moon Press
The Spring Journey to the Saxon Shore, pub. Equinox Press
Spitting Pips pub. Equinox Press
Business in Eden pub. Equinox Press
Marching with Tulips, pub. Alba
What Happens in Haibun, pub. Alba
The Humours of Haiku, pub. Iron Press
Haiku, pub. British Museum Press

The above obtainable at www.davidcobb.co.uk

Also, now out-of-print:

A Bowl of Sloes, pub. Snapshot Press
The Iron Book of British Haiku, pub. Iron Press

Of possible interest:

Haiku in the British Isles: a Tale of Acceptance and Non-Acceptance, in: Hugh Cortazzi (ed.) *Britain and Japan: Biographical Portraits, Vol. IX* pub. Renaissance Books for the Japan Society